W9-BCM-186

FREEDOM'S PROMISE

THE MAKING OF MOTOWN

BY DUCHESS HARRIS, JD, PHD

WITH REBECCA ROWELL

Core Library

An Imprint of Abdo Publishing
abdobooks.com

Cover image: The Temptations were a popular Motown
group in the 1960s.

abdocorelibrary.com

Published by Abdo Publishing, a division of ABDO, PO Box 398166, Minneapolis, Minnesota 55439. Copyright © 2019 by Abdo Consulting Group, Inc. International copyrights reserved in all countries. No part of this book may be reproduced in any form without written permission from the publisher. Core Library™ is a trademark and logo of Abdo Publishing.

Printed in the United States of America, North Mankato, Minnesota
092018
012019

Cover Photo: Granamour Weems Collection/Alamy
Interior Photos: Granamour Weems Collection/Alamy, 1; Gilles Petard/Redferns/Getty Images, 5, 19; Donaldson Collection/Michael Ochs Archives/Getty Images, 6–7, 43; Bob Dear/AP Images, 10; AP Images, 14–15; Val Wilmer/Redferns/Getty Images, 20; PF1/WENN/Newscom, 22–23; GAB Archives/Redferns/Getty Images, 26; Leroy Patton/Ebony Collection/AP Images, 28; Michael Ochs Archives/Getty Images, 30–31; Red Line Editorial, 32, 39; Archive Photos/Paramount Pictures/Moviepix/Getty Images, 36–37

Editor: Maddie Spalding
Series Designer: Claire Vanden Branden

Library of Congress Control Number: 2018949710

Publisher's Cataloging-in-Publication Data

Names: Harris, Duchess, author. | Rowell, Rebecca, author.
Title: The making of Motown / by Duchess Harris and Rebecca Rowell.
Description: Minneapolis, Minnesota : Abdo Publishing, 2019 | Series: Freedom's promise | Includes online resources and index.
Identifiers: ISBN 9781532117718 (lib. bdg.) | ISBN 9781641856058 (pbk) | ISBN 9781532170577 (ebook)
Subjects: LCSH: Motown Productions--Juvenile literature. | Popular music record industry--Juvenile literature. | Record music industry--Juvenile literature.
Classification: DDC 338.76178--dc23

CONTENTS

A LETTER FROM DUCHESS

Every generation has its sound. One of the sounds of the 1960s was Motown. The Motown record label was important in American music because it did more than create big hits. Motown responded to the politics of the time. It led teens of all races to join together for social change.

The founder of Motown, Berry Gordy, is quoted as saying, "I recognized the bridges that we crossed, the racial problems and the barriers that we broke down with music. . . . We would go back and the audiences were integrated and the kids were dancing together and holding hands."

As you think about the impact of music, ask yourself, "What is the soundtrack for my generation?"

Please join me in learning about Motown's impact on America. Come with me on a journey that tells the story of the promise of freedom.

Motown legends the Four Tops signed with the record label in the 1960s.

A SUPREME PERFORMANCE

On July 29, 1965, three young African American women stood before the audience at the Copacabana, a popular nightclub in New York City. Diana Ross, Mary Wilson, and Florence Ballard were part of a singing group called the Supremes. The nightclub could fit 650 people, and it was full. The audience included celebrities and people who regularly visited the club. Many of these people were white and middle aged. This was not the Supremes' typical audience.

The Motown group the Supremes became widely popular in the 1960s through both live and televised performances.

7

THE STYLISH SUPREMES

As the Supremes gained popularity, their look became more sophisticated. They wore sequined gowns and wigs of different hairstyles. Fake eyelashes, large earrings, and makeup helped them look dramatic and elegant. Gordy wanted to make the group unique among girl groups. Other girl groups at the time had different styles. The Shirelles had a simple fashion style, not fancy. The Ronettes wore bold clothes. The trendsetting Supremes became the definition of glamour.

But they cheered as the Supremes took their places.

THE COPACABANA

The Supremes were a Motown group. Their songs featured the Motown sound. The songs were mostly happy, and they were rhythmic with a heavy beat. The music made listeners want to move and dance.

The Supremes were not the first black singers to perform at the Copacabana. But they were the first artists from Motown to play there. Though the South was known for segregation, the practice was also common in the North, including in New York City restaurants. Until the club integrated in 1957, the Copacabana had not allowed black customers. Even eight years later, the Copacabana's audience was primarily white.

The Supremes' songs were already popular among both black and white audiences. But the Supremes' manager, Berry Gordy Jr., knew this would be an important show for the group. The Copacabana was a long way from the group's humble beginnings. The nightclub would hopefully be a stepping stone to the best venues in the United States.

THE SUPREMES

Ross, Wilson, and Ballard had grown up together in the 1940s and 1950s. Their families had all lived in the Brewster-Douglass Housing Projects in Detroit, Michigan. These housing projects were for working-class and poor families. The three young women had started singing together in 1959. Gordy signed the women

The Supremes had many hit songs in the 1960s.

to his record company in 1961. He named them the Supremes.

The Supremes became Gordy's prized act. The group skyrocketed to fame. They had three major hit singles in 1964. "Where Did Our Love Go," "Baby Love," and "Come See about Me" all topped the pop music charts. In 1965 "Stop! In the Name of Love" and "Back in My Arms Again" became top hits.

The popularity of the Supremes' 1964 releases earned them an appearance on *The Ed Sullivan Show* in December of the same year. Performing on the widely watched television show strengthened the group's popularity, including with white Americans. The *Ed Sullivan* performance was part of Gordy's plan to make Motown's music and artists mainstream, appealing to black and white audiences alike. Gordy carefully crafted the sound and the people of Motown.

Gordy spent four months preparing the Supremes for their gig at the Copacabana. The singers learned show tunes that would appeal to a white audience. Gordy wanted to satisfy the tastes of white Americans while also giving them something new.

SUCCESS

The Supremes crooned into their microphones, opening their set with several songs from popular musicals.

Next the Supremes sang three of their own songs. The remainder of the set was more non-Motown music.

The performers' elegant style and clothing fit in at the high-class club, and the mix of pop music and show tune standards was perfect for the audience. The nightclub filled with applause. The Supremes were a hit. And just as Gordy expected, their successful performance opened doors. They began to play major venues, including return engagements at the Copacabana.

Motown music appealed to both black and white audiences when American society was still largely segregated. Motown helped change white people's idea of black music, made black music mainstream, and launched the careers of many black performers. In the process, Gordy proved that a black man could be a successful businessman. And it all began with an idea and $800.

EXPLORE ONLINE

Chapter One discusses the Motown group the Supremes. The article at the website below goes into more depth on this topic. Does the article answer any questions you had about the Supremes? Does it provide any new information that interests or surprises you?

THE STORY OF THE SUPREMES
abdocorelibrary.com/making-of-motown

BERRY GORDY AND MOTOWN RECORDS

Motown music originated in Detroit, Michigan. Gordy founded Tamla Records there in January 1959. Gordy's family loaned him $800 to start the company. One of Tamla's labels was called Motown Records. Gordy named it after his hometown. Detroit was called the "Motor City" because car manufacturing was the city's main industry. Gordy thought of Detroit as more of a town than a city because of the friendly relationships he had with his neighbors.

Berry Gordy, *right*, helped launch the careers of many musicians, including Smokey Robinson, *left*.

DETROIT IN THE EARLY 1900s

In the early 1900s, African Americans living in the South began moving to the North. They were looking for a better life. The South had few job opportunities. It also had segregation laws. World War I (1914–1918) created a need for workers in the North. Between 1910 and 1920, the black population of Detroit grew 611 percent. In the North, African Americans did not face legal segregation. But they were still affected by racism. Racist housing practices created segregated neighborhoods. People in white neighborhoods had better opportunities. Racism restricted education and job opportunities for black people.

Gordy made "Motor Town" into a single word, Motown.

GORDY'S BACKGROUND

Gordy was born in Detroit in 1929. He started writing songs when he was only seven years old. Gordy dropped out of high school to become a boxer. He was a successful athlete. But he knew that boxers were often injured. He decided to return to his passion, music. He wanted to be a songwriter.

Gordy's musical career was put on hold when the US Army drafted him in 1951 to fight in the Korean War (1950–1953). He served two years in the military and then returned to Detroit. Next, he opened a record store, but the business did not last long.

In 1955 Gordy got a job at a car company. He worked for Ford on an assembly line, fastening upholstery. The job was boring, but he mentally composed songs as he worked. After a few years, Gordy quit. He still dreamed of being a songwriter.

Gordy's music career got a boost when he met Jackie Wilson at the Flame Show Bar. The bar was a popular hangout for singers and songwriters. Wilson was an African American R&B singer. Gordy started writing songs for Wilson. Some became hits in the late 1950s.

Hoping to build on his successes, Gordy started a music publishing company, Jobete. But Jobete was not very profitable. So Gordy launched Tamla Records, still hoping to break into the music industry. The office for his record company was in a two-story house on West Grand Boulevard. Gordy and his wife lived on the second floor. He turned the garage into a recording studio. He put a sign over the front door with the office name, "Hitsville USA."

GORDY'S VISION

Gordy was not the first African American to own a music company. Selling music by black artists was also not

Gordy sits in his office in Detroit in the 1960s.

new. But selling that music to white customers was new. So was getting pop radio stations to play records by black artists.

Music was categorized based on the color of the artists performing it. Songs labeled as R&B when black artists performed them were called pop music when white artists performed them. Often, songs first performed by African Americans became popular among white audiences only after white performers covered them. One famous example is Elvis Presley's "Hound Dog." It was a big hit in 1956. Willie Mae

Willie Mae "Big Mama" Thornton was an African American blues singer and musician.

"Big Mama" Thornton, an African American singer, originally recorded the song.

Gordy wanted to make music for everyone. He signed his first group in 1959. It was the Miracles, led by Smokey Robinson. In 1960 Gordy founded Motown Record Corporation. It became the parent company of Motown Records and Tamla Records. That same year, Motown had its first hit. The company was off to a good start. With Gordy's vision and oversight, Motown would soon take off.

STRAIGHT TO THE
SOURCE

Gordy knew before he started a record company what he wanted to achieve. In 2016 he explained his plan in an interview for the British newspaper the *Telegraph*:

> *I wanted to have a kid off the street walk in one door unknown and come out another door a star, like an assembly line; that was my dream. My family said, that's stupid. Those are cars. You can't do that with human beings. I said, well it's the same thing—the artists come in and you have one group writing the songs and producing them, then somebody else works on their stage performance and so on. People would say, well, that's never been done before. Well, maybe that's the reason we should do it!*

Source: Mick Brown. "Berry Gordy: The Man Who Built Motown." *Telegraph*. Telegraph Media Group Limited, January 23, 2016. Web. Accessed July 21, 2018.

What's the Big Idea?

Take a close look at this passage. How is Gordy's idea for creating musical stars similar to producing cars? How do you think this mindset helped him make Motown successful?

VAN DYK

THE MOTOWN MACHINE

Gordy created what became known as the Motown sound. He produced music people could easily dance to. It grabbed listeners' attention. The songs took their style from blues, gospel, pop, and swing. Then Gordy added a heavy beat. Songs often included tambourines and handclapping. Horns were in the mix too. Gordy also liked to use string instruments such as violins. It was a new trend, and Gordy joined in.

Gordy relied heavily on a group of jazz musicians when composing and recording. The group was called the Funk Brothers.

A group called the Funk Brothers provided backup music for Motown songs during recording sessions.

LESSONS IN GOOD BEHAVIOR

Maxine Powell was Motown's head of artist development. She taught the label's many young artists how to behave. That included how to walk, sit, stand, talk to fans and the media, and dress. Lessons were twice a week. Attendance was required. Powell's lessons also covered performing. She helped Marvin Gaye stop singing with his eyes closed. She told her students they would be good enough to perform for royalty.

They became Motown's in-house band. Other people, including Robinson, wrote lyrics. Motown songs often talked about love or heartbreak.

Motown often tried different artists or different versions of a song to find the right mix of performer and arrangement. Gordy approached his company like an assembly line. He found a style that worked, repeated it, and made records as fast as possible.

Gordy also applied the assembly line practice of quality control. Before a car could go out the door, it had to be inspected for quality. At Motown, this took the form of a meeting every Friday. Producers and songwriters attended these meetings. They presented their songs for review. Then everyone at the meeting would vote. Only the favorite songs were released. But Gordy had the final say.

Gordy's factory approach applied to the artists too. Motown developed stars. Artists worked with a voice coach and a choreographer. They also got lessons in good manners. The lessons were part

PERSPECTIVES

MOTORTOWN REVUE

In the 1960s, Motown sent a group of artists on a tour through the United States. The tour was called the Motortown Revue. Some tour stops were in the South. The black artists encountered racism there. Most public places were segregated. In some towns, the performers did not get a warm welcome. Instead, they were faced with police officers and dogs. The Supremes' Diana Ross said of the experience: "In some of those Southern towns, you could just feel the bigotry in the air. You could slice it with a knife like stinking cheese."

of Gordy's plan to create music to appeal to all people. He wanted the artists themselves to be appealing.

PROMOTION

Gordy created great music and artists. Next he needed to get Motown records into the hands of pop radio disc jockeys and onto record store shelves. He needed to sell, distribute, and promote the music Motown made.

In 1961 Gordy hired Barney Ales to help with the business side of Motown. Ales had experience in sales, distribution, and promotion. He had worked for Capitol and Warner Brothers, two major record companies. Ales's job at Motown was to get the company's music on the radio and in record stores. As a white man, Ales helped Motown bridge the racial divide.

For several years, Motown's salesmen were all white. In 1969 Ales hired Miller London as the company's first African American salesman. Ales would

Motown singer Marvin Gaye, *left*, poses with Barney Ales, *right*, in 1969.

Gordy worked closely with artists such as the Jackson 5 to create great music.

continue to hire black men to sell Motown's records,

further integrating Motown's own sales team and the

pop music business.

STRAIGHT TO THE
SOURCE

Martha Reeves was the lead singer of Martha and the Vandellas, a popular Motown group in the 1960s. In a 2011 interview, Reeves spoke about Gordy and the purpose of Motown music:

> From the very first day of my arrival, I noticed that there was always a line, people wanting to be on the label, and people wanting to be . . . discovered by [Berry] Gordy. . . . I know not only that our music [makes] you feel good, but we also had a message of equality. We had a message of actually enjoying music. And I don't think our music was designed for any particular people, any particular race or creed or color or age. It's just the sound of young America, and that's what was in our label, and that's what we take pride in.

> Source: "Motown: A Game-Changer for Black Americans." *NPR*. NPR, February 23, 2011. Web. Accessed July 22, 2018.

Consider Your Audience

Adapt this excerpt for a different audience, such as your parents or friends. Write a blog post conveying the same information for the new audience. How does your post differ from the original text, and why?

MOTOWN'S SUCCESS AND LATER YEARS

Motown's successes came quickly. In 1961 the Miracles' song "Shop Around" became Motown's first gold record. Another popular early Motown group was the Marvelettes. Their song "Please Mr. Postman" became Motown Records' first number one song on the pop music charts.

In 1961 Gordy signed the Temptations and the Supremes. The singers in both groups were teenagers. In a few years, they would become stars. An 11-year-old singer named Stevie Wonder also joined Motown Records in 1961.

The Jackson 5 were among Motown's most popular artists in the 1960s and 1970s.

1960s MOTOWN HITS

Artist	Song	Year Released
The Marvelettes	"Please Mr. Postman"	1961
The Supremes	"Baby Love"	1964
The Temptations	"Get Ready"	1966
Marvin Gaye	"Heard It Through the Grapevine"	1968
The Jackson 5	"I Want You Back"	1969

Motown had dozens of number one songs on the pop charts in the 1960s. Listed above are some of the most famous ones. Search for these songs online and listen to them. What are they about? Do you notice any common themes?

Other artists who joined Motown in the 1960s included the Four Tops, Marvin Gaye, and the Jackson 5. They all had successful careers as Motown artists.

For many of its artists, Motown felt like a sort of home. The people involved in the company supported each other like family. But the world was changing, and Motown's music would too.

TIME OF PROTEST

Motown music became popular at the height of the American civil rights movement. African Americans were fighting for their rights. They protested segregation and inequality. At the same time, many people also were protesting the Vietnam War (1954–1975). They wanted US troops to leave Vietnam. Motown music would soon evolve to fit within this period of mass protest and change.

PERSPECTIVES

MARY WILSON

During the 1960s, racial tension was at a peak as African Americans and supporters pushed for civil rights. Mary Wilson of the Supremes explained the importance of Motown during this troubling time period: "We represented a social environment that was changing. The experience we had known being black was not being bona fide citizens, not being able to drink out of the same water fountains, playing to segregated audiences. When that started to fall away, and you saw that music was one of the components that was helping it fall away, that's when it really felt like we were doing something significant."

In the late 1960s and early 1970s, songs about love and heartbreak were still popular. But some new Motown songs reflected the tensions in society. Motown singer Edwin Starr released his chart-topping song "War" in 1970. It reflected the frustrations many people felt about the Vietnam War. The song's message is that war causes destruction and has no purpose.

Gaye also released an antiwar song. "What's Going On" peaked at number two on the pop music charts in April 1971. The song's emotions came from the pain Gaye saw his brother experience while fighting in Vietnam. Gordy did not understand the song and did not want to release it. But Gaye insisted, threatening to stop recording for Motown. The song was a big success.

NEW MOTOWN SOUNDS

In the early 1970s, other artists also sought to break out of Motown's mold. Wonder had gained fame at a young age. By 1972 he started to write his own music. Wonder wrote or cowrote and produced all the songs for his album *Talking Book*. It includes "Superstition" and "You Are the Sunshine of My Life," which both hit number one on the charts.

The Jackson 5 had great success in the early 1970s. Their most popular songs included "ABC" and "Dancing Machine." Other artists joined the Motown family in the 1970s. One successful group was the Commodores. The group's biggest single was "Three Times a Lady." During this time, Gordy made a major change to Motown. It affected Motown's location and its existence.

BLACK FORUM

A new Motown label, Black Forum, started in 1970. Black Forum sold records featuring oral history, poetry, and speeches. Gordy worried that the label would make Motown look political and hurt the success of popular acts. Still he created the label. But audiences were attracted to Motown's music, not speeches. Gordy ended the label in 1973 because it was not making money.

MOTOWN'S LEGACY

n 1972 Gordy moved Motown's headquarters to Los Angeles, California. He formed a film production company called Motown Productions. From 1975 to 1985, Motown Productions made seven films. The first was *Lady Sings the Blues*. The film tells the story of African American jazz singer Billie Holiday. Diana Ross played the lead role. She was nominated for an Oscar for her performance.

Moving to California did not make Motown more successful. It did the opposite. After the move, Gordy focused on movies, not music. Some lead singers of Motown groups

Motown singer Diana Ross, *right*, starred in films for Motown Productions including *Lady Sings the Blues*.

left their groups to begin solo careers. Some artists changed labels.

In 1988 Gordy sold Motown to MCA for $61 million. Today, Universal Records owns the company. It is called Universal Motown. Stevie Wonder remains one of its artists.

HONORING MOTOWN LEGENDS

On January 20, 1988, popular musicians from the past and present gathered in New York City. Some among them were being inducted into the Rock

MOTOWN TIMELINE

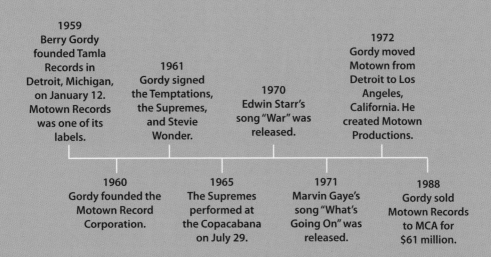

1959
Berry Gordy founded Tamla Records in Detroit, Michigan, on January 12. Motown Records was one of its labels.

1960
Gordy founded the Motown Record Corporation.

1961
Gordy signed the Temptations, the Supremes, and Stevie Wonder.

1965
The Supremes performed at the Copacabana on July 29.

1970
Edwin Starr's song "War" was released.

1971
Marvin Gaye's song "What's Going On" was released.

1972
Gordy moved Motown from Detroit to Los Angeles, California. He created Motown Productions.

1988
Gordy sold Motown Records to MCA for $61 million.

The above timeline gives some key events in Motown's history. How does this timeline help you understand Motown's legacy?

and Roll Hall of Fame. It was the third occasion of this annual event.

Inductees were legends in the music business. They included the Beatles and Bob Dylan. The Supremes were being honored too. The Supremes were one of Motown's most popular groups. They were the top female group of the 1960s. Their induction into the

MOTOWN THE MUSICAL

In April 2013, a new musical opened on Broadway in New York City. *Motown the Musical* tells the story of Gordy's life and career. The show includes more than 50 Motown songs. A national tour ran for four years. During that time, more than 5 million theatergoers experienced the joy of Motown. The musical brought people together to enjoy music, much as the Motortown Revue had done in the 1960s.

Rock and Roll Hall of Fame was a major achievement for Motown Records.

Gordy was also honored that night. He was inducted in the nonperformer category for founding Motown. He brought black music to pop radio. Under his direction, Motown earned acclaim across the country and across racial lines. Motown was the first African American–owned record label to achieve such broad success. Gordy had forever changed music.

Motown may no longer exist today as it did in the 1960s, but its legacy lives on. Hitsville USA, the original home of Motown, is now a museum. Visitors can experience the space the way their favorite artists did. And Motown's songs are ready to play whenever people want to enjoy them. When they do listen, they are hearing more than the Motown sound. They are listening to history.

FURTHER EVIDENCE

Chapter Five talks about the Motown Museum and the legacy of Motown music. What was one of the main points of this chapter? What evidence is included to support this point? Read the article at the website below. Does the information on the website support the main point of the chapter? Or does it present new evidence?

MOTOWN HISTORICAL MUSEUM
abdocorelibrary.com/making-of-motown

FAST FACTS

- In 1959 Berry Gordy founded Tamla Records in Detroit, Michigan. One of its labels was Motown Records.

- Gordy helped create famous acts such as Smokey Robinson and the Miracles, the Temptations, the Supremes, Marvin Gaye, and Stevie Wonder.

- Motown artists topped the charts in the 1960s.

- In 1972 Gordy moved Motown to Los Angeles, California. He established Motown Productions and got into the movie business. Motown Productions created movies starring Motown singer Diana Ross.

- Gordy sold Motown Records in 1988 for $61 million.

- Gordy was inducted into the Rock and Roll Hall of Fame in 1988.

STOP AND
THINK

Tell the Tale

Chapter One of this book discusses the Supremes' 1965 performance at the Copacabana nightclub. Imagine that you were in the audience at this concert. Write 200 words about your experience. What did you observe? How did the audience react?

Why Do I Care?

The Motown period spanned many years, from the 1960s through the 1980s. How does Motown affect your life and other people's lives today? How might life today be different without Motown's legacy?

Dig Deeper

After reading this book, what questions do you still have about Motown? With an adult's help, find a few reliable sources that can help you answer your questions. Write a paragraph about what you learned.

GLOSSARY

bigotry
an unwillingness to accept
members of a particular
group of people

cover
to record or perform a
song another artist has
already recorded

drafted
chosen by the government
for military service

gold record
a record that has sold
500,000 copies

induct
to make a person or a
group an official member of
an organization

integrate
to include people of
all races in a group in
an attempt to give them
equal rights and protection
under the law

label
a company that creates and
sells recordings of music

parent company
a company that owns
other companies

segregate
to separate people of
different races or ethnic
groups through separate
schools and other
public spaces

ONLINE
RESOURCES

To learn more about the making of **Motown**, visit our free resource websites below.

Visit **abdocorelibrary.com** for free Common Core resources for teachers and students, including vetted activities, multimedia, and booklinks, for deeper subject comprehension.

Visit **abdobooklinks.com** for free additional online weblinks for further learning. These links are routinely monitored and updated to provide the most current information available.

LEARN
MORE

Anniss, Matt. *The Story of Soul and R&B*. Mankato, MN: Smart Apple Media, 2014.

Winter, Max. *The Civil Rights Movement*. Minneapolis, MN: Abdo Publishing, 2015.

ABOUT THE
AUTHORS

Duchess Harris, JD, PhD

Professor Harris is the chair of
the American Studies department
at Macalester College and curator
of the Duchess Harris Collection of
ABDO books. She is the author and
coauthor of recently released ABDO
books including *Hidden Human
Computers: The Black Women
of NASA*, *Black Lives Matter*, and *Race
and Policing*.

Before working with ABDO, she authored several other books on the
topics of race, culture, and American history. She served as an associate
editor for *Litigation News*, the American Bar Association Section of
Litigation's quarterly flagship publication, and was the first editor in
chief of *Law Raza*, an interactive online journal covering race and the
law, published at William Mitchell College of Law. She has earned a PhD
in American Studies from the University of Minnesota and a JD from
William Mitchell College of Law.

Rebecca Rowell

Rebecca Rowell has put her degree in publishing and writing
to work as an editor and an author of many books for Abdo
Publishing. Her recent books include *Emmanuel Macron* and
The American Middle Class (coauthored with Duchess
Harris). Rowell lives in Minneapolis, Minnesota.

INDEX